W9-CMS-212

The Stars

Carmel Reilly

Marshall Cavendish
Benchmark
New York

This edition first published in 2012 in the United States of America by
Marshall Cavendish Benchmark
An imprint of Marshall Cavendish Corporation

All rights reserved.

No part of this publication may be reproduced, stored in a retrieval system or transmitted, in any form or by any means, electronic, mechanical, photocopying, recording, or otherwise, without the prior permission of the copyright owner. Request for permission should be addressed to the Publisher, Marshall Cavendish Corporation, 99 White Plains Road, Tarrytown, NY 10591. Tel: (914) 332-8888, fax: (914) 332-1888.

Website: www.marshallcavendish.us

This publication represents the opinions and views of the author based on Carmel Reilly's personal experience, knowledge, and research. The information in this book serves as a general guide only. The author and publisher have used their best efforts in preparing this book and disclaim liability rising directly and indirectly from the use and application of this book.

Other Marshall Cavendish Offices: Marshall Cavendish International (Asia) Private Limited, 1 New Industrial Road, Singapore 536196 • Marshall Cavendish International (Thailand) Co Ltd. 253 Asoke, 12th Flr, Sukhumvit 21 Road, Klongtoey Nua, Wattana, Bangkok 10110, Thailand • Marshall Cavendish (Malaysia) Sdn Bhd, Times Subang, Lot 46, Subang Hi-Tech Industrial Park, Batu Tiga, 40000 Shah Alam, Selangor Darul Ehsan, Malaysia

Marshall Cavendish is a trademark of Times Publishing Limited

All websites were available and accurate when this book was sent to press.

Library of Congress Cataloging-in-Publication Data

Reilly, Carmel, 1957-
  The stars / Carmel Reilly.
     p. cm. — (Sky watching)
  Includes index.
  Summary: "Provides scientific information about the stars"—Provided by publisher.
  ISBN 978-1-60870-583-2
  1. Stars—Juvenile literature. 2. Astronomy—Observers' manuals—Juvenile literature. I. Title.
  QB801.7.R45 2012
  523.8—dc22
                                2010044018

Publisher: Carmel Heron
Commissioning Editor: Niki Horin
Managing Editor: Vanessa Lanaway
Project Editor: Tim Clarke
Editor: Paige Amor
Proofreader: Helena Newton
Designer: Polar Design
Page layout: Romy Pearse
Photo Researcher: Legendimages
Illustrator: Adrian Hogan
Production Controller: Vanessa Johnson

Printed in China

Acknowledgments
The author and publisher are grateful to the following for permission to reproduce copyright material:

Front cover photograph: Milky Way stars in dawn sky © Dreamstime/Rastan.

Photographs courtesy of: Australian Astronomical Observatory, photograph by David Malin, © 1989-2010, **22**; Dreamstime/Diebar, **5** (centre inset), /Rastan, **1**; iStockphoto/Mike Sonnenberg, **5** (bottom), /Sergii Tsololo, border element throughout; NASA, /CXC, MIT, F.K.Baganoff et al, **23**; NASA, ESA and AURA/Caltech, **13**; NASA, ESA, K. Noll (STScI), **28**; NASA/ESA/SOHO, **14**, /JPL-Caltech, **19**, /JPL-Caltech/J. Hora (Harvard-Smithsonian Center for Astrophysics), **18**, /Lunar and Planetary Laboratory, **5** (top); Photolibrary/ Photo Researchers, **21**, /Radius Images, **27**, /RKN, **10**, /Babk Tafreshi, **8**; Shutterstock/Wolfgang Kloehr, **11**.

While every care has been taken to trace and acknowledge copyright, the publisher tenders their apologies for any accidental infringement where copyright has proved untraceable. They would be pleased to come to a suitable arrangement with the rightful owner in each case.

Please Note
At the time of printing, the Internet addresses appearing in this book were correct. Owing to the dynamic nature of the Internet, however, we cannot guarantee that all these addresses will remain correct.

CONTENTS

Glossary Words

Words that are printed in **bold** are explained in the glossary on page 31.

What Does It Mean?

Words that are within a **box** are explained in the "What Does It Mean?" panel at the bottom of the page.

SKY WATCHING

When we sky watch, we look at everything above Earth. This includes what is in Earth's **atmosphere** and the objects we can see beyond it, in space.

Why Do We Sky Watch?

Sky watching helps us understand more about Earth's place in space. Earth is our home. It is also a planet that is part of a space neighborhood called the **solar system**. When we sky watch we learn about Earth, and our neighbors inside and outside the solar system.

What Objects Are in the Sky?

There are thousands of objects in the sky above Earth. These are Earth's neighbors—the Sun, the Moon, planets, stars, and flying space rocks (**comets**, **asteroids**, and **meteoroids**). Some can be seen at night and others can be seen during the day. Although some are visible with the human eye, all objects must be viewed through a telescope to be seen more clearly.

When and How Can We See Objects in the Sky?

Object in the Sky	Visible with Only the Human Eye	Visible Only through a Telescope	Visible during the Day	Visible at Night
Earth's Atmosphere	✗	✗	✗	✗
Sun	✓ (Do not view directly)	✗ (View only with a special telescope)	✓	✗
Moon	✓	✗	Sometimes	✓
Planets	Sometimes	Sometimes	Sometimes	✓
Stars	Sometimes	Sometimes	✗	✓
Comets	Sometimes	Sometimes	✗	✓
Asteroids	Sometimes	Sometimes	✗	✓
Meteoroids	Sometimes	Sometimes	✗	✓

WHAT DOES IT MEAN ? **space** The area in which the solar system, stars, and galaxies exist, also known as the universe.

THE STARS

Stars are space objects that can be seen in the sky with the human eye. Stars are visible at night, but not during the day, apart from our Sun. Our Sun is a star, but it can only be seen during the day.

Star Watching

People have always watched the stars. However, it was only after telescopes were invented 500 years ago that **astronomers** could finally see them more clearly. Now, because of space exploration and space science, people know much more about the stars. Today people now know what they are made of, how they are born and die, and how they can affect Earth.

Sky watching can be done during the day or night, with or without a telescope. Just look up!

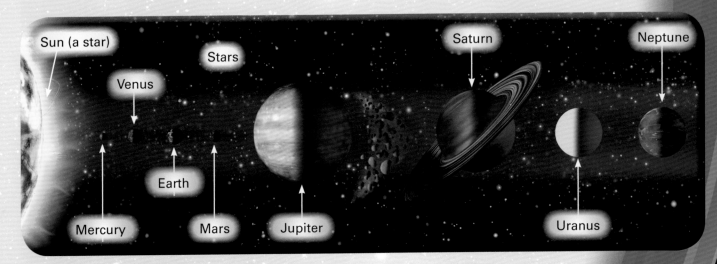

Stars can be found everywhere in space. The Sun is a star. This diagram shows the approximate relative sizes of the Sun and the planets. The distances between them are not to scale.

WHAT ARE STARS?

Stars are formed from clouds of **gas** and dust floating in space. They are huge balls of gas that give out energy.

Stars Are Formed from Gas and Dust

Stars begin life as clouds of gas and dust called a **nebula**. Gravity then pulls the nebula together. The nebula begins to spin and forms a hot ball of gas, called a **protostar**. Over millions and even billions of years, this protostar slowly forms into a star.

4. A huge ball of hot gases, called a protostar, forms at its center. Cooler dust and gases spin around the outside.

3. The nebula begins to spin and grow very hot.

5. The dust and gases flatten into a spinning disc.

2. The pull of gravity begins to shrink the nebula and brings it together.

1. A star begins life as a swirling nebula.

6. The ball of hot gases in the center becomes a star. Planets and other space objects form from the dust that spins around it.

FAMOUS SKY WATCHERS

French mathematician Pierre-Simon de Laplace developed the nebular theory in the late 1700s. He put forth the idea that our Sun and solar system began with a huge, shrinking, gas nebula.

It takes billions of years for stars like our Sun to form.

WHAT DOES IT MEAN ?

gravity The force that attracts all objects toward each other.

Stars Produce Energy

Stars are huge balls of gas that give off energy in the form of heat and light. They do this by a process called nuclear fusion. Stars are made up mostly of **hydrogen**. In nuclear fusion, the particles of hydrogen join together and make another gas called **helium**. When this happens, energy is given off as heat and light.

Star Fact

Stars emit huge amounts of energy. Our Sun is a medium-sized star. Every second the Sun gives out about the same amount of energy as 2 billion power plants could produce in a year.

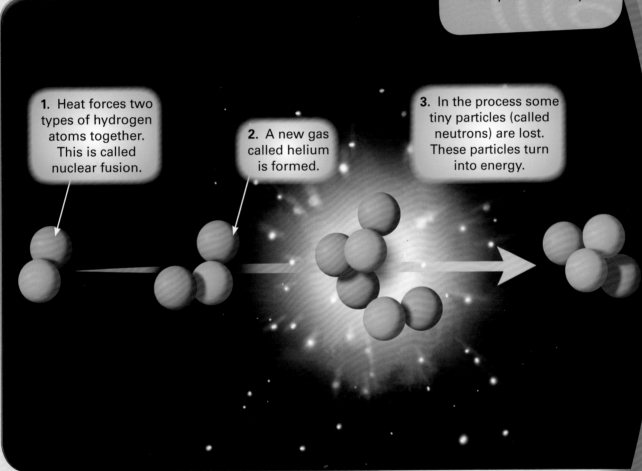

1. Heat forces two types of hydrogen atoms together. This is called nuclear fusion.

2. A new gas called helium is formed.

3. In the process some tiny particles (called neutrons) are lost. These particles turn into energy.

The intense heat inside stars is what allows nuclear fusion to begin.

WHAT DOES IT MEAN

nuclear fusion   A process that releases energy when two or more atoms (the smallest part of substance) join together to form a single new atom.

WHAT DO STARS LOOK LIKE FROM EARTH?

From Earth, stars look like tiny, twinkling lights in the night sky. However, our closest star, the Sun, looks very different. It is a giant ball of light in the daytime sky.

Stars Look Like Thousands of Points of Light

At night we see thousands of stars in the night sky. They seem tiny because they are so far away. However, many are as big as our Sun.

V Alpha Centauri is a star seen in the night sky. It is billions of times farther away from Earth than the Sun.

Alpha Centauri

Star Fact

The distance from Earth to stars is measured in light-years. This is the time it takes for light to travel in a year. The nearest star to our Sun is Alpha Centauri. It is 4.3 light-years away.

Stars Twinkle

Stars seem to twinkle in the night sky. This is because of the atmosphere around Earth. Stars are far away, which means their light is faint. When this light reaches Earth, it has traveled through the atmosphere, which is always moving. As the atmosphere moves, the light from stars is carried in different directions. This makes the stars seem to twinkle.

FAMOUS SKY WATCHERS

In 1838, German astronomer Friedrich Bessel became the first person to measure the distance between Earth and a star outside our solar system. Over his lifetime, he made a list of the positions of more than 50,000 stars.

Light from a star

Earth's atmosphere

Wind and weather move the atmosphere.

The light from stars bends as it passes through the atmosphere. This makes stars appear to be twinkling.

Our Sun Is a Star

The star we can see most clearly from Earth is the Sun. All stars are like the Sun and give out heat and light. However, not all stars are as large as the Sun.

WHAT ARE STARS MADE OF?

Scientists have discovered that stars are made of gases. They have a core of hot, thick gas. This is surrounded by two layers of cooler gas and a surface, called a photosphere.

Stars Have a Core

The center of a star is called the core. Although the core is small, it is heavy because it is full of tightly packed gases. The core is where energy is made by nuclear fusion.

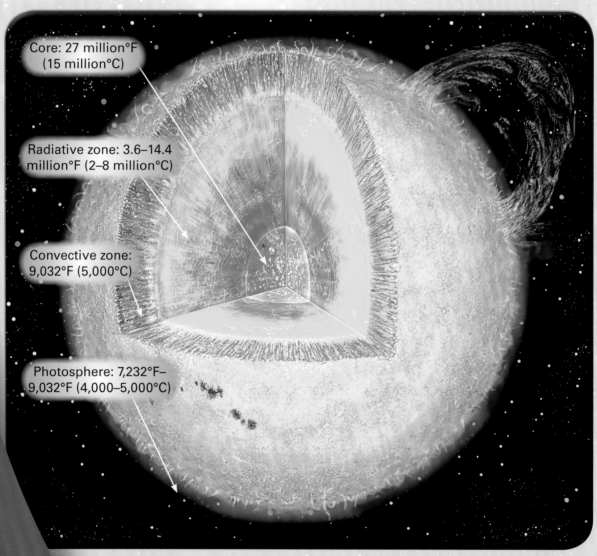

Core: 27 million°F (15 million°C)

Radiative zone: 3.6–14.4 million°F (2–8 million°C)

Convective zone: 9,032°F (5,000°C)

Photosphere: 7,232°F– 9,032°F (4,000–5,000°C)

This is the make-up of our Sun, which is a typical star.

Stars Have Two Layers of Gas around the Core

Stars have two layers of cooler gases that lie between the core and the surface. They are called the radiative and convective zones. Energy made in the core travels very slowly through these zones to the star's surface.

Stars Have a Surface

The surface of a star is called the photosphere. This is where the star's energy flows out into space. The photosphere is also the beginning of a star's atmosphere. A lot of solar activity takes place in this zone.

V It can take hundreds of thousands of years for energy from the core to reach a star's surface. It is this energy we see shining from stars billions of miles away.

Star Fact

Conditions on the surface of a star are violent. The heat from the center of a star boils up on the photosphere. Stars send out huge spikes, called spicules, and loops of gas, called prominences. They can reach thousands of miles into space.

ARE ALL STARS THE SAME?

Stars come in many colors, temperatures and sizes. Astronomers can find a star's temperature and age by looking at its light. Astronomers group stars according to their color and luminosity. Most stars are main sequence stars, some sit in clusters, and many are in pairs, known as binary stars.

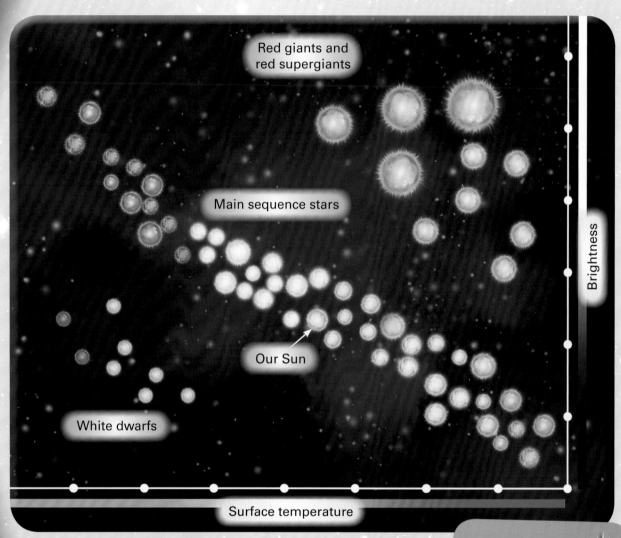

Red giants and red supergiants

Main sequence stars

Our Sun

White dwarfs

Brightness

Surface temperature

 A graph called a Hertzsprung–Russell diagram helps astronomers place stars into particular groups. This is done by plotting a star's brightness against its temperature, as well as noting its color.

WHAT DOES IT MEAN

luminosity The amount of energy given off by a star in the form of brightness.

Star Fact

Small yellow or orange stars live for longer than large blue or white stars. This is because large stars burn their fuel about ten times faster than small stars.

Most Stars Are Main Sequence Stars

Stars begin their lives as main sequence stars. They burn hydrogen in their cores, creating nuclear fusion. Some of these stars are average in size and some are huge. Main sequence stars are grouped by astronomers according to the colors they give out. Stars that look blue and white are the hottest. Yellow, orange, and red stars are the coolest.

The Hottest Stars Are Blue and White

Blue and white stars are the hottest main sequence stars. Smaller bluish-white stars have a surface temperature from about 13,532°F to 18,032°F (7,500°C – 10,000°C). The surface of larger, brighter blue stars can be as hot as 108,032°F (60,000°C).

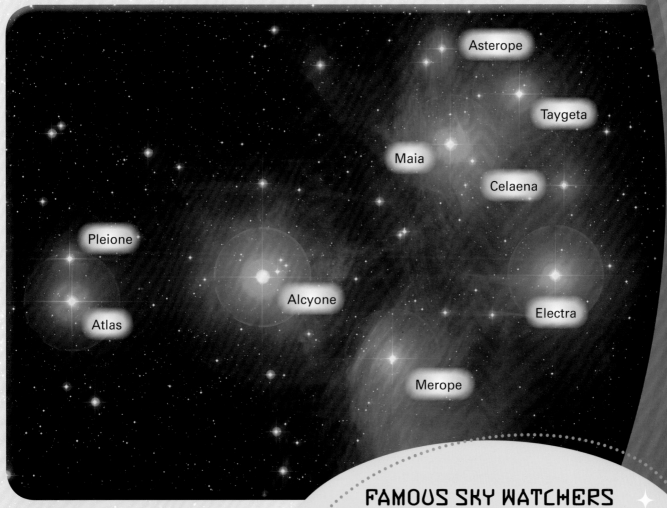

Asterope

Taygeta

Maia

Celaena

Pleione

Alcyone

Electra

Atlas

Merope

∧ This group of blue-white stars is called the Pleiades. These stars are about 375 light-years from Earth.

FAMOUS SKY WATCHERS

Cecilia Payne-Gaposchkin was a British-American astronomer who studied the temperature of stars. In 1925 she became the first astronomer to suggest that hydrogen was the most common element within a star.

Cooler Stars Are Yellow, Orange, and Red

Yellow, orange, and red stars have cooler surface temperatures than blue or white stars. The hottest of the yellow stars has a surface temperature of about 13,532°F (7,500°C). Orange stars have a surface temperature of between 6,332°F and 9,032°F (3,500°C – 5,000°C). Red stars are the coolest, at between 3,632°F and 9,032°F (2,000°C – 3,500°C).

Some Stars Are Part of a Cluster

Astronomers have found many large groups, or clusters, of stars in our galaxy and even beyond. They are known as global clusters and open star clusters.

Gravity Brings Global Clusters Together

Global clusters are large groups of stars that are held together by their own gravity. These groups of stars are very old and often have millions of members.

V Our Sun is a yellow main sequence star. It has a surface temperature of about 11,732°F (5,500°C).

Open Star Clusters Are Groups of Young Stars

Open star clusters are young stars that were all formed from the same nebula. As these stars grow older, they move farther apart.

Many Stars Are Binary Stars

Many stars are double stars, or binary stars. They are stars that **orbit** each other. Astronomers believe that more than half of the stars in the galaxy are binary stars.

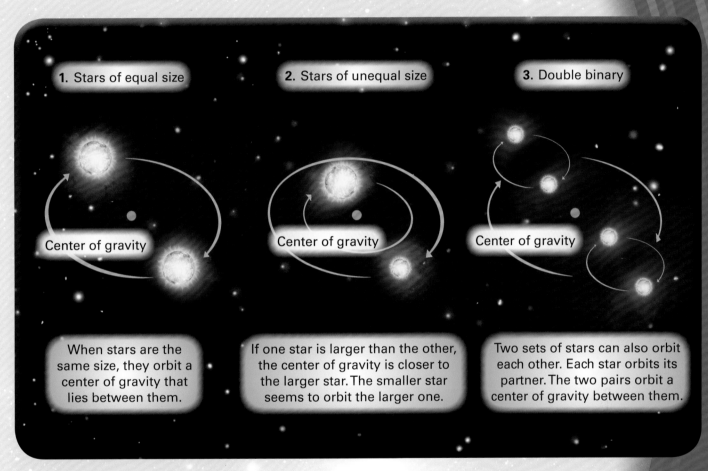

1. Stars of equal size

2. Stars of unequal size

3. Double binary

Center of gravity

Center of gravity

Center of gravity

When stars are the same size, they orbit a center of gravity that lies between them.

If one star is larger than the other, the center of gravity is closer to the larger star. The smaller star seems to orbit the larger one.

Two sets of stars can also orbit each other. Each star orbits its partner. The two pairs orbit a center of gravity between them.

There are different types of binary stars. They can change from one to another as they grow older. Some stars orbit so close that gases can pass between them.

FAMOUS SKY WATCHERS

The earliest known observation of a double, or binary star, was made by Giovanni Riccioli in 1650. Using a telescope, he was able to see that Mizar, which is a star in the **constellation** of Ursa Major, was not one but two stars.

WHAT ARE THE STAGES IN THE LIFE OF A STAR?

Stars spend most of their lives as main sequence stars. As smaller to medium-sized main sequence stars come to the end of their lives, they turn into red giants. When red giants start to die, they cast off their outer layers in the form of **planetary nebula**. What is left behind is called a white dwarf.

Larger main sequence stars become supergiants. Supergiants later become supernovas. They turn into neutron stars or black holes.

V Our Sun is an average main sequence star. Billions of years from now it will become a red giant and finally a white dwarf star.

FAMOUS SKY WATCHERS

Since the late nineteenth century, much of what we know about stars has come from the work of mathematicians and physicists. The theories of physicists like Albert Einstein and Niels Bohr have helped scientists figure out many things about stars, including the stages of their lives and how long they might live.

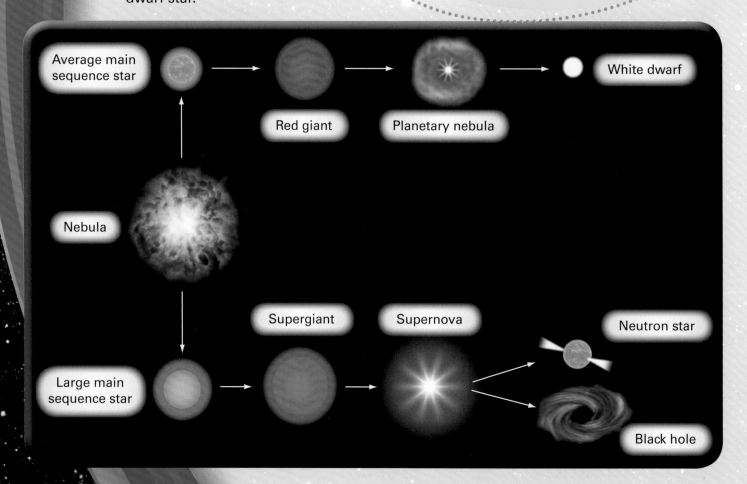

Average main sequence star → Red giant → Planetary nebula → White dwarf

Nebula

Large main sequence star → Supergiant → Supernova → Neutron star / Black hole

Stars Begin as Main Sequence Stars

Main sequence stars change hydrogen into helium to create energy. Stars spend most of their lives in this form. When the hydrogen in a star starts to run out, the star must start using its helium. When this happens, the star begins to change.

Smaller Main Sequence Stars Turn into Red Giants

As a smaller main sequence star starts to burn its helium, it can become as much as 100 times larger and brighter. A star at this stage is called a red giant. As the red giant runs out of helium, it begins to change again. Its core shrinks and its outer shell falls away.

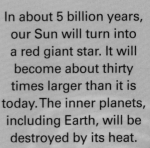

Star Fact

In about 5 billion years, our Sun will turn into a red giant star. It will become about thirty times larger than it is today. The inner planets, including Earth, will be destroyed by its heat.

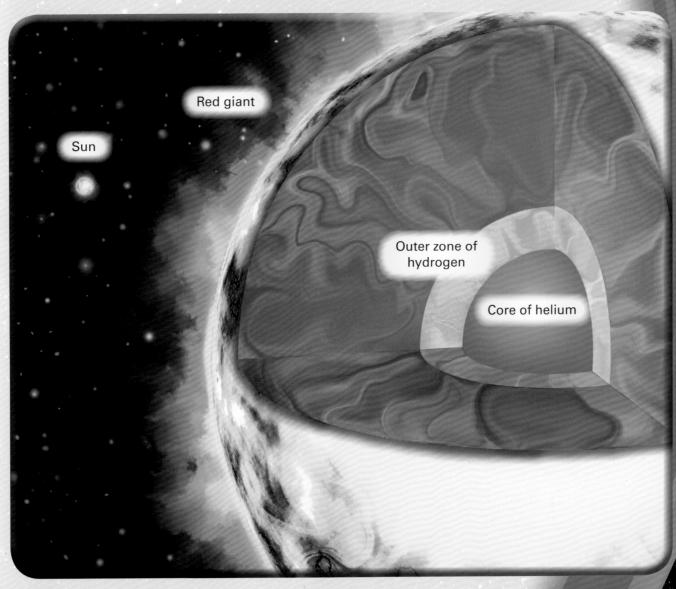

Red giant

Sun

Outer zone of hydrogen

Core of helium

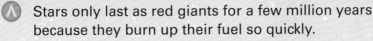 Stars only last as red giants for a few million years because they burn up their fuel so quickly.

Red Giants Shed Their Outer Layer

When a red giant's shell falls away, gas is left behind. This gas is lit up by the hot core underneath. The glowing gas is called a planetary nebula. Planetary nebulas last for a few thousand years.

Gases

Core that will become a white dwarf star

A planetary nebula is made of gas that is given off by a red giant star before it becomes a white dwarf. This one is called the Ring Nebula and it is located about 2,000 light-years from Earth.

FAMOUS SKY WATCHERS

In 1781, the German-British astronomer William Herschel was the first to use the term "planetary nebula." This is what he called the clouds he could see forming in space. He did not realize they were collapsing stars. He thought they looked like huge planets.

White Dwarfs Remain

When the planetary nebula blows away, the core of the star is left behind. This core is called a white dwarf star. A white dwarf is very hot and **dense**. Its temperatures can be as high as 180,032°F (100,000°C). Because white dwarf stars are small and faint, only those closest to Earth can be seen. A white dwarf cannot make its own energy, which is why it gradually cools down and fades away.

V This white dwarf is called G29–38. It began as a star that was about three times as large as our Sun.

Star Fact

The **matter** in white dwarf stars is very dense and heavy. If a white dwarf were the size of a cell phone, it would be as heavy as a large elephant.

Larger Main Sequence Stars Turn into Supergiants

The largest main sequence stars become supergiants. They are much larger than red giant stars. Supergiants can be up to 1,000 times bigger than our Sun. They are different colors depending on their heat. Supergiants end their lives as supernovas, which are huge, colorful explosions.

Star Fact

Most red giant stars last for one or two billion years. At most, supergiant stars will live for thirty million years.

Supergiants Are Different Colors

The color of a supergiant depends on how hot it is. Like smaller stars, supergiants can be blue, white, yellow, or red. Blue supergiants are the hottest. Red supergiants are the coolest.

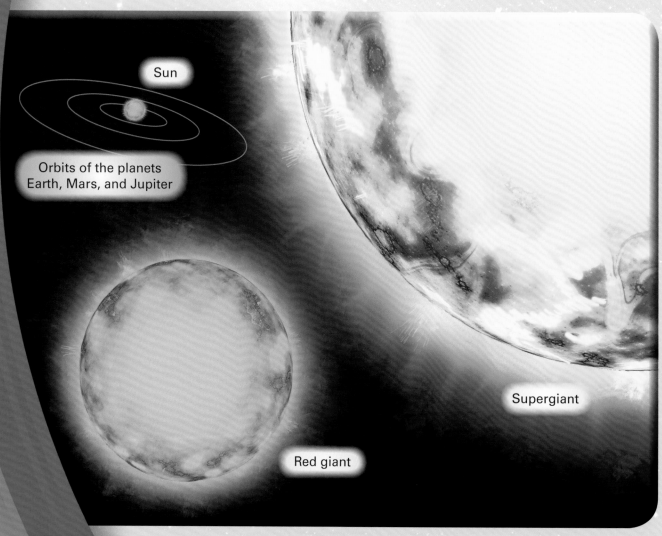

Sun

Orbits of the planets Earth, Mars, and Jupiter

Supergiant

Red giant

If a supergiant were at the center of our solar system instead of the Sun, it would reach as far as the planet Mars.

Supergiants Grow Hotter and Heavier

Supergiant stars are larger than other stars, which is why they burn up their helium more quickly. They grow extremely hot because of their size and because they have huge amounts of helium to burn. The intense heat inside them allows them to create heavy elements at their core, like iron. The core finally becomes so heavy that it collapses under its own weight. This sends a shockwave through the star that leads to an explosion called a supernova.

Mu Cephei

Mu Cephei is one of the largest and brightest supergiant stars that can be seen from Earth.

FAMOUS SKY WATCHERS

The supergiant star Mu Cephei has been observed by many astronomers. It was named in the 1600s by Johann Bayer. In 1783, William Herschel studied the star and made note of its red color. In 1843, John Hind discovered that it is a variable star, which means that it changes in brightness.

Supergiants Turn into Supernovas

When a supergiant explodes, it becomes a supernova. A supernova is extremely hot and glows very brightly for a few days. As the supernova expands, its glow begins to fade. A supernova can last for a few weeks or for hundreds of years.

Supernova 1987A Could Be Seen for Eighty-Five Days

In February 1987, a supernova appeared from a blue supergiant star. It was in a galaxy close to the **Milky Way**, called the Large Magellanic Cloud. Over the next eighty-five days, the supernova became larger and brighter. It was so bright that it could be seen from Earth without a telescope.

blue supergiant

FAMOUS SKY WATCHERS

In 1572, Danish astronomer Tycho Brahe gave supernovas their name. Not knowing what he was really observing when he first saw one, he called it a *nova* (or new) star.

⋀ The photo on the left shows the blue supergiant before it exploded. The photo on the right shows it after it exploded and became Supernova 1987A.

22

Some Supernovas Turn into Neutron Stars

After a supernova fades, the core of the star is left behind. This is a tiny, dense object called a neutron star. Neutron stars are not made of gas. They have iron crusts and liquid centers. They are so heavy that their gravity is thousands of times stronger than that of a main sequence star.

Some Supernovas Turn into Black Holes

When a very large star dies, a black hole can be created. A black hole forms where a star's core used to be. Its gravity is so strong that nothing falling within its range can escape from it. A black hole looks black because its pull of gravity is so strong that even light cannot escape it.

V Scientists believe this super-massive black hole is at the center of the Milky Way. It is called Sagittarius A* and everything in the galaxy orbits around it.

Star Fact

A neutron star is about the size of a small city, but weighs as much as the Sun. Some neutron stars are so heavy that they collapse under their own weight and become black holes.

Do Stars Move?

Stars move in two ways. They orbit the galaxy as they travel through space. At the same time, each star **rotates** on its **axis**.

Stars Orbit the Center of the Galaxy

There are billions of stars in our galaxy, the Milky Way. These stars, along with all the other objects in the galaxy, orbit a point of gravity at the galaxy's center.

(V) Some parts of the galaxy move more quickly than others. The part of our galaxy where the Sun lies moves at around 155 miles (250 kilometers) per second.

Star Fact

Stars in the Milky Way travel at between 124 and 155 mi. (200 and 250 km) per second. Even at these speeds it takes them hundreds of thousands of years to complete their orbit of the galaxy.

The arms are made up of stars, gas, and dust

Central galactic bulge (galaxy's center)

Sagittarius Arm

124 mi. (200 km) per second

Orion Arm

155 mi. (240 km) per second

Our Sun

149 mi. (240 km) per second

137 mi. (220 km) per second

Perseus Arm

Stars Rotate

Each of the stars in our galaxy rotates on its axis. It takes our Sun about one month to fully rotate. However, some stars can rotate in just a few hours. Some parts of the same star rotate at different speeds.

Some Parts of a Star Rotate Faster than Others

Because a star is made of gas, some parts of it rotate more quickly than others. Gas at the top and bottom of a star takes longer to rotate than gas near the star's equator . The inner part of the Sun rotates at about the same speed as its equator.

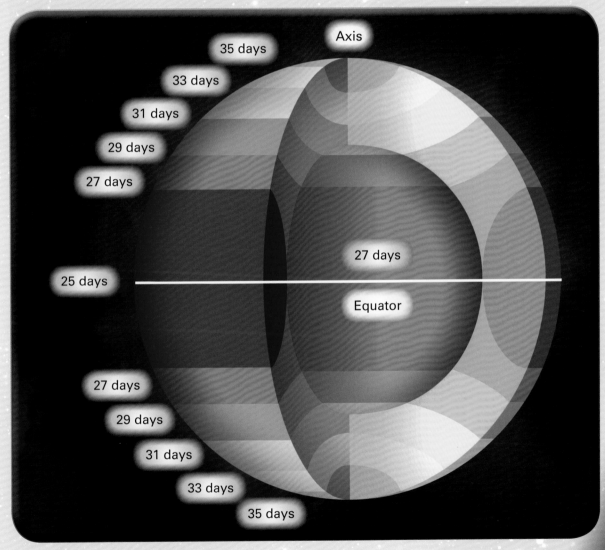

 The Sun is like all stars. Different parts of it rotate at different speeds.

WHAT DOES IT MEAN ?

equator An imaginary line around the middle or widest part of a space object, such as a star or planet.

HOW DO STARS AFFECT EARTH?

One star, the Sun, affects our planet enormously. Without it, Earth would not exist. Other stars do not directly affect Earth, but they have always been an important part of life on our planet.

Star Fact

For thousands of years, travelers have used the stars to help them get around at night. From the position of the stars, you can find north, south, east, and west.

Stars, such as the Sun provide the energy that allows life to exist.

Without our star, the Sun, Earth would not exist. The Sun's energy helped to create life on Earth.

People have always watched the distant stars, using them as guides and mapping the constellations.

Energy from the Sun Helped Create Earth

Earth was created from gas and dust orbiting the Sun billions of years ago. The Sun's energy helped to create life on Earth. Earth's atmosphere uses the heat of the Sun to keep the planet warm.

What If There Were No Stars?

If there were no Sun, life on Earth would not exist. There would not be any energy to provide heat and light. Without a Sun, Earth itself would never have formed. Without other stars, the nighttime sky would be very dark and drab.

The Distant Stars Help Us Find Our Way

Although the distant stars have no direct effect on Earth, they have always played an important part in life on the planet. People have always been curious about the stars. In ancient times, people made maps of the stars. The stars are also used in **navigation**, especially at sea. Stars are also featured in the music, stories, poetry, and art of all cultures around the world.

What If There Were No Stars?

If there were no distant stars, there would be no change to the planet Earth itself. However, life on Earth would be a little different. The night skies would be dimmer, and would not have been used for navigation. Stars would also not be featured in art and storytelling.

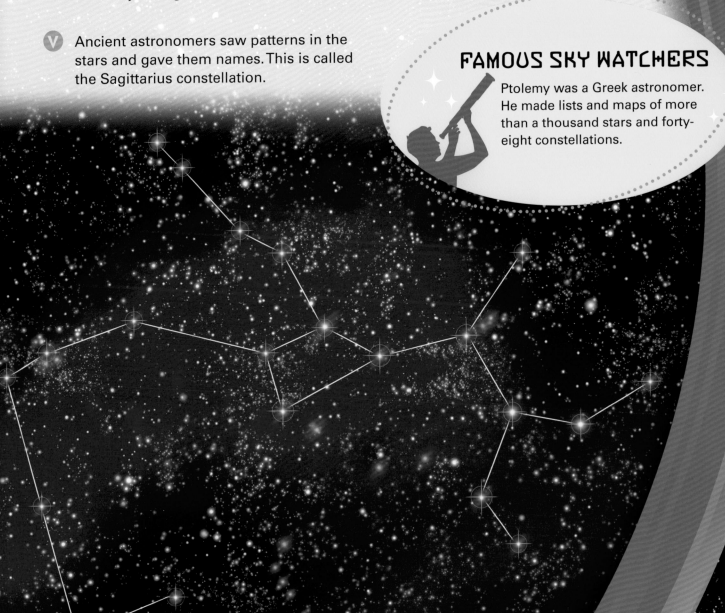

V Ancient astronomers saw patterns in the stars and gave them names. This is called the Sagittarius constellation.

FAMOUS SKY WATCHERS

Ptolemy was a Greek astronomer. He made lists and maps of more than a thousand stars and forty-eight constellations.

WHAT DOES THE FUTURE HOLD FOR STARS?

Most of the stars in space are so large that almost nothing can destroy them. Stars are born, have long lives, and die. However, even death is not really the end for stars.

Almost Nothing Can Destroy Stars

Most stars are so large that their gravity catches smaller space objects. These smaller objects usually go into orbit around the star. Some are pulled toward the star and are destroyed on impact. The only thing strong enough to destroy a star is a black hole.

But Stars Can Die

Most stars live long lives. As they use up their hydrogen fuel, they begin to die. Red giants become white dwarfs and fade away. Over millions of years, they become colder and crumble away. The same thing happens to neutron stars that are formed from supergiants.

Star Fact

Our Sun and solar system are made of matter left over from older stars and space objects. When our Sun dies, the matter left behind will go toward forming new stars.

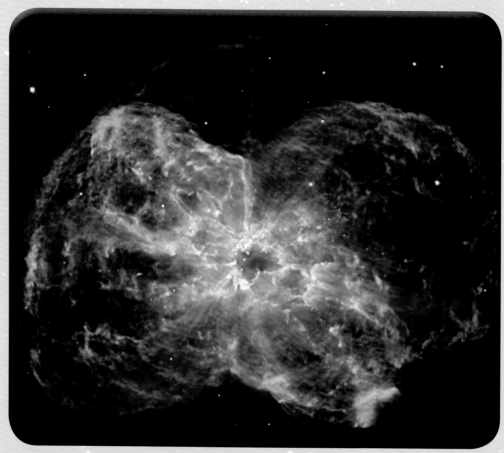

All of the matter from stars breaks down and returns to space as gas and dust.

New Stars Form

Matter is given off by a dying star. It forms a cloud of gas and dust called a nebula. A nebula floats in space, gathering more matter. When it grows large, it starts to develop gravity. Gravity pulls the nebula together. As it is pulled together, the nebula starts to spin and a new star begins to form.

3. A huge ball of hot gases, called a protostar, forms at its center. Cooler dust and gases spin around the outside.

The gas and dust left over from stars is used to build new stars.

2. The pull of gravity begins to shrink the nebula and brings it together. It begins to spin and grow very hot.

1. At first there is a swirling nebula.

FAMOUS SKY WATCHERS

American astronomer and photographer Henry Draper was the first person to photograph a nebula. In 1870 he photographed the Orion Nebula. It is the brightest nebula we can see from Earth.

WHAT ARE THE BEST WAYS TO STAR-WATCH?

Stars can be seen with the human eye on a clear night. If you use binoculars or a home telescope, you will be able to see more stars.

Star Watching at Home

To watch the stars at home, you will need a map of the night sky and binoculars or a telescope. Choose just one part of the sky that you can see from the map. Can you match the stars you see with your eyes with those on the map? Now look at the same part of the sky using binoculars. Can you see more stars?

Star Watching Online

Research more about the stars online. What can you learn about the stars you can see in your part of the world from these websites? The Your Sky website is a good place to start (see below).

Useful Equipment for Backyard Astronomy

Equipment	What It Is Used for
Binoculars or a Telescope	A pair of binoculars or a telescope will help you see more stars.
Star Map	A star map will help you to identify the stars and constellations you can see.
Compass	A compass will help you face the right direction when reading star map.
Flashlight with Red Cellophane over the Lightbulb	Use a flashlight to help you read the star map. Putting red cellophane over the lightbulb end of the flashlight will prevent its light from affecting your night vision.

Useful Websites

Star Child: http://starchild.gsfc.nasa.gov/docs/StarChild/StarChild.html

Stars: http://imagine.gsfc.nasa.gov/docs/science/know_l2/stars.html

Stars: www.enchantedlearning.com/subjects/astronomy/stars

Your Sky: http://fourmilab.ch/yoursky/

Glossary

asteroids	Small, rocky, or metal space objects that orbit the Sun.
astronomers	People who study stars, planets, and other bodies in space.
atmosphere	The layer of gases that surrounds a planet, moon, or star.
axis	An imaginary line through the middle of an object, from top to bottom.
comets	Small, rocky, and icy space objects that have long, shining tails that appear when orbiting near the Sun.
constellation	A group of stars that seem to form a pattern in the night sky.
dense	Heavy for its size.
equator	An imaginary line around the middle or widest part of a round space object, such as a star or planet.
galaxy	A large system of space objects, including stars, planets, gas, and dust.
gas	A substance that is not solid or liquid, and is usually invisible.
gravity	The force that attracts all objects toward each other.
helium	An air-like substance that is colorless and odorless; the second most common gas in the universe.
hydrogen	An air-like substance that is colorless, odorless, and can easily catch on fire; the most common gas in the universe.
luminosity	The amount of energy given off by a star in the form of brightness.
matter	A substance of a particular kind, such as gas and dust.
meteoroids	Small space objects that are made of rock and metal, ranging from several feet wide to the size of a pea.
Milky Way	The galaxy that is home to our solar system.
navigation	The process of working out a position and plotting a route to follow.
nebula	A cloud of gas and dust in space.
nuclear fusion	A process that releases energy when two or more atoms (the smallest part of substance) join together to form a single new atom.
orbit	To travel around another, larger space object.
planetary nebula	An outer layer of gas that is thrown off by a star in its last stages of life.
protostar	A young star, in the form of a cloud of gas and dust, that has not yet started to create energy in its core.
rotates	Turns or spins around a fixed point or an axis, like a spinning top.
solar system	The Sun and everything that orbits it, including planets and other space objects.
space	The area in which the solar system, stars, and galaxies exist, also known as the universe.

INDEX

2 1982 03027 1823

JUN   2013